Just Little Things

A Celebration of Life's Simple Pleasures

Nancy Vu

A Perigee Book

A PERIGEE BOOK
Published by the Penguin Group
Penguin Group (USA) Inc.
375 Hudson Street, New York, New York 10014, USA

USA / Canada / UK / Ireland / Australia / New Zealand /
India / South Africa / China

Penguin Books Ltd., Registered Offices: 80 Strand, London
WC2R 0RL, England
For more information about the Penguin Group,
visit penguin.com.

Library of Congress Cataloging-in-Publication Data

Vu, Nancy.
Just little things : a celebration of life's simple pleasures /
Nancy Vu.
pages cm
"A Perigee book."
ISBN 978-0-399-16297-8
1. Simplicity. 2. Joy. 3. Happiness. 4. Pleasure. I. Title.
BJ1496.V82 2013
646.7—dc23   2012049846

First edition: May 2013

PRINTED IN THE UNITED STATES OF AMERICA

10 9 8 7 6 5 4 3

While the author has made every effort to provide
accurate telephone numbers, Internet addresses, and other
contact information at the time of publication, neither the
publisher nor the author assumes any responsibility for
errors, or for changes that occur after publication. Further,
the publisher does not have any control over and does
not assume any responsibility for author or third-party
websites or their content.

Introduction

One of my favorite things in the world is listening to my grandmother tell a story about her past. In particular, I love to watch her eyes—the delicate crevices around them, and the way they glisten with passion and nostalgia. Watching and listening to her not too long ago, I realized that it's the small details that bring us the most joy.

Too often in our fast-paced world, these details go unnoticed, overshadowed by the stress and obligations of our daily routines. I believe we can shift our perceptions of life, and rediscover happiness, by paying attention to these simple, everyday details. The little things.

Toward the end of 2010, I created a blog—JustLittleThings.net—consisting of colorful posts cataloging the small joys in life. After only a few entries, which included things like "a hot shower on a cold day," "long road trips at night," and "your favorite song on replay," the posts began to reach a wide audience. I started to receive dozens of messages from people expressing their gratitude for brightening their day or making them smile. The blog was also able to help people cope with rough times in their lives. After reading a few telling me that my simple blog helped them fight disease and even stopped some from self-harm and suicide, I knew for sure that little things can indeed make a big difference. Over a short period of time, the blog has grown tremendously, now with nearly half a million readers from all over the world.

There are so many little glimmers of joy buried under life's routines and troubles; we just have to open our eyes and minds in order to notice them. I hope that the "little things" on these pages help you shift your perspective. As you read them, I invite you to take a step back, look around, and appreciate every little thing that life has to offer, no matter how small it may seem.

A compliment from a stranger.

Going to bed knowing you can sleep for as long as you want.

Seeing the sun rise and set.

The smell of fresh-baked bread.

Finding something you lost.

When a friend
enjoys something
you recommended.

A full fridge after grocery shopping.

Sleeping in your own bed after being away.

Lemonade on a hot day.

Making a
baby laugh.

Hearing an old song you used to love.

The fresh, clean feeling after taking a shower.

When a little kid reaches up to hold your hand.

Taking off your shoes and socks after a long day.

Overhearing someone say nice things about you.

When you talk to an old friend and it's like nothing has changed.

The feeling of sand between your toes.

Being told you are appreciated.

Changing into pajamas after coming home from a formal event.

Flipping to a new month on your calendar.

The first flavorful chews of a new piece of gum.

The sound of a perfect high five.

When someone genuinely asks you how your day was.

Finally eating the food you've been craving.

Looking at old photographs.

Instant friendships.

Being looked up to as a role model.

The smell of the air after it rains.

Finishing a really good book.

Sleeping on freshly washed sheets.

The warmth of the sun on your face.

Finally arriving at your destination after a long journey.

When people enjoy the food you make.

Realizing your hiccups are gone.

When your favorite store has a sale.

Clean public restrooms.

The brief moment of silence when you drive under an overpass on a rainy day.

Handwritten letters.

Your pet's excitement when you come home.

Good dreams.

When a person's laugh is funnier than the joke.

Getting something right on the first try.

Having something to look forward to.

Wearing brand-new clothes.

When the lights start to dim before a movie begins.

Beating your high score.

The first day of the year it's warm enough to wear sandals.

When your favorite movie is on television.

Being able to breathe through your nose after a cold.

Going through
all the photos you
took at the end
of the day.

The color of people's eyes.

Being told your advice was helpful.

Tossing something in the trash and making it in.

The feel of your hair when you wash out the conditioner.

When you don't
have to wait in line.

The cold side of the pillow.

Knowing all the words to a song.

Revisiting old childhood places.

When someone
remembers
the things you like.

Being ahead of schedule.

Accents.

Walking into an air-conditioned building after being outside in the heat.

Being surrounded by people you love.

When a song starts
to play right when
you turn on the radio.

Using brand-new markers.

Hearing crumbs getting sucked up by the vacuum cleaner.

Arriving at the bus stop right on time.

The sound of birds chirping in the morning.

Having time for yourself.

When you and
a friend say the
same thing at the
same time.

The first step into a warm bath.

Finding money in your pocket.

The first drop of a rollercoaster.

Surprising people with a talent they never knew you had.

Having your favorite meal for dinner.

Being praised for something you put a lot of time and effort into.

When the power comes back after an outage.

Stargazing.

Accomplishing something before the microwave beeps.

Contagious laughter.

When a baby falls asleep in your arms.

Writing with a freshly sharpened pencil.

Discovering something you forgot you had.

Freckles.

Old couples holding hands.

When someone tells you that you smell nice.

The sound a
soda can makes
when you open it.

Getting into your freshly washed car.

Accelerating after being in a traffic jam.

When someone replies instantly.

Treating yourself to a guilty pleasure.

Arriving on time when you thought you wouldn't.

Realizing your bad haircut has grown out.

Trying something on and discovering it fits perfectly.

Singing in the shower.

Perfectly peeling off a price sticker.

Hearing people cheer for you.

People who love what they do for a living.

The sound
of the ocean.

When someone stands up for you.

The first snowfall.

When you see
your food coming
at a restaurant.

When someone brings you back a souvenir.

Peeling an orange in one piece.

When you finally remember the word you had on the tip of your tongue.

Learning a new song on a musical instrument.

The first signs
of spring.

Spontaneous adventures.

Being told you've made someone's day.

When your hair
stays where you
want it to.

Looking at water droplets travel across your car window.

Coming up with
a good idea.

Handmade gifts.

Getting paid.

Opening a brand-new book.

When the other person hugs back tighter.

Witnessing a child's firsts.

Releasing a sneeze.

Making a great catch.

The smell of popcorn in a movie theater.

Being treated like family when you're not.

Writing on the first page of a notebook.

Achieving the perfect milk to cereal ratio.

When people remember your birthday.

Free stuff.

Watching old home videos.

The warmth of freshly printed paper.

When someone is excited to see you.

When the wind blows your hair in the right direction.

Finding something to add to your collection.

The sound of crackling firewood.

When your online order finally arrives.

Collapsing on your bed after a long day.

Sweater weather.

The satisfaction of scratching an itch.

Finding a curly fry mixed in with your regular fries.

Cool summer breezes.

Waking up and realizing your bad dream wasn't real.

City lights at night.

When someone says "bless you" after you sneeze.

Seeing your parents smile at each other.

Seeing leaves change color in the fall.

Watching a new episode of your favorite TV show.

When your pet cuddles up next to you.

The sound of a little kid's uncontrollable laughter.

Seeing bus drivers wave to each other.

Continuous green lights when you're driving.

When the team you're rooting for wins.

Naps.

Seeing your breath on cold days.

When someone spells your name correctly.

Silence that isn't awkward.

Remembering there are good leftovers from the day before.

Finding the person you're looking for in a crowd.

Seeing dough rise in the oven.

Crossing things off your to-do list.

A smile from a stranger.

Discovering that something is within your price range.

The fresh feeling after brushing your teeth.

Seeing sunlight shining through tree leaves.

Your favorite part of a song.

Drawing on a foggy window.

Falling asleep to the sound of rain.

When everybody's in a good mood.

The feel of freshly shaved skin.

Bonding with someone you never expected to.

Wrapping your cold hands around a warm drink.

When a stranger helps you pick up something you dropped.

Accomplishing something people thought you couldn't.

Cold showers in the summer.

A stream of good songs in a row.

Seeing a rainbow after a storm.

Finally finding a comfortable sleeping position.

When someone understands your humor.

Listening to your grandparents tell stories.

Wearing your pajamas all day.

Random acts of kindness.

The smell of fresh laundry.

Being taken care of when you're sick.

Rereading your favorite book.

Walking to the beat of the song you're listening to.

Popping bubble wrap.

The first swim of the summer.

Dimples.

Finding the perfect gift.

Being unable to finish a sentence because you're laughing so hard about the ending.

Realizing you have more time to get things done than you thought.

When people are protective of you.

Putting in the last few pieces of a puzzle.

When someone
you haven't seen
in a long time still
remembers you.

Crawling back into a warm bed.

Waking up on your birthday.

Hearing someone refer to you as a friend for the first time.

The first sip from
a can of soda.

The sound of fallen autumn leaves crunching under your feet.

Hearing interesting stories about yourself when you were little.

Teaching someone a new skill and seeing their face light up when they get it.

Reuniting with your family after being away from home for a while.

Quality bonding time.

Getting the window seat on an airplane.

Taking a perfect picture.

Seeing a baby yawn.

Finally seeing someone you've missed.

Eating cookies still warm from the oven.

Being the bearer of good news.

A hug when you need one most.

The smell of
old books.

The way hair looks underwater.

An inspiring conversation with a stranger.

Late-night summer drives.

Arriving at a new place without getting lost.

The way babies smell.

The first bite of food when you're really hungry.

The smell of your favorite scented candle.

When the vending machine finally accepts your dollar bill.

Remembering the name of the song that's been stuck in your head.

The sound of birds singing in the morning.

The feeling after a good workout.

**Going through
an old box full of
childhood things.**

When a stranger
thanks you for
holding the door.

Tears of joy.

Waking up and realizing you have more time to sleep.

Seeing elderly people full of life.

Finally releasing your laughter after trying to hold it in.

**The night before
your favorite holiday.**

Lighting candles during a power outage.

When someone comes running to hug you.

Discovering a new song and instantly loving it.

Winning a bet.

The first sip of coffee in the morning.

Hearing that you were in someone's dream.

Opening a new box of crayons.

Waking up to the sun shining through your window.

Parking your car
at the same time a
song ends.

Drinking cold water when you're really thirsty.

A good stretch after sleeping.

When people remember you after meeting you only once.

Effortless conversations.

Coming home to the smell of good cooking.

When someone puts a blanket over you while you're asleep.

Finally getting out what was stuck in your teeth.

When the last pair of shoes in stock is your size.

Getting a compliment you've never received before.

Seeing someone use a gift you gave them.

Getting lost in a book.

Feeling accomplished at the end of the day.

Making someone laugh really hard.

Looking back and realizing how far you've come.

Acknowledgments

I am indebted to the love and support from my family. I am eternally grateful for my parents, especially, who have shaped the person I am today. I cannot think of anyone else who would have raised me better than my mom and dad.

A heartfelt thanks and appreciation to my friends and the faculty members at Presentation High School for cheering me on every step of the way in the making of this book.

A big thanks to my editor, Marian Lizzi, who discovered the *Just Little Things* blog and believed I was doing something really special. Thank you for this great opportunity and for your invaluable advice.

Of course, this book would not have been possible without the rest of the staff at Perigee Books, including the publisher, John Duff, and the art director, Lisa Amoroso.

A special thank-you to all of my *Just Little Things* blog readers for your kind words, motivating support, and thoughtful suggestions. I want to express my deep appreciation for all of your heartwarming messages and emails that left me feeling truly touched. I am very grateful for your contributions in sharing my blog posts and spreading the message of my blog to others. *Just Little Things* would not have been as successful as it is now if it were not for your unyielding support.

Thank you so much, everyone!